MAKING THE FINAL 32

THE ROAD TO THE
WORLD'S MOST POPULAR
CUP:

THE ROAD TO THE
WORLD'S MOST POPULAR
CUP

MAKING
THE FINAL 32

Andrew Luke

MASON CREST

MASON CREST

450 Parkway Drive, Suite D | Broomall, Pennsylvania 19008
(866) MCP-BOOK (toll-free)

Andrew Luke

First printing
9 8 7 6 5 4 3 2 1

ISBN (hardback) 978–1-4222–3954–4
ISBN (series) 978–1-4222–3949–0
ISBN (ebook) 978–1-4222–7832–1

Cataloging-in-Publication Data on file
with the Library of Congress

QR CODES AND LINKS TO THIRD-PARTY CONTENT

You may gain access to certain third-party content ("Third-Party Sites") by scanning and using the QR Codes that appear in this publication (the "QR Codes"). We do not operate or control in any respect any information, products, or services on such Third-Party Sites linked to by us via the QR Codes included in this publication, and we assume no responsibility for any materials you may access using the QR Codes. Your use of the QR Codes may be subject to terms, limitations, or restrictions set forth in the applicable terms of use or otherwise established by the owners of the Third-Party Sites. Our linking to such Third-Party Sites via the QR Codes does not imply an endorsement or sponsorship of such Third-Party Sites or the information, products, or services offered on or through the Third-Party Sites, nor does it imply an endorsement or sponsorship of this publication by the owners of such Third-Party Sites.

CONTENTS

KEY ICONS TO LOOK FOR:

Words to Understand: These words with their easy-to-understand definitions will increase the reader's understanding of the text while building vocabulary skills.

Sidebars: This boxed material within the main text allows readers to build knowledge, gain insights, explore possibilities, and broaden their perspectives by weaving together additional information to provide realistic and holistic perspectives.

Educational videos: Readers can view videos by scanning our QR codes, providing them with additional educational content to supplement the text. Examples include news coverage, moments in history, speeches, iconic sports moments, and much more!

Text-Dependent Questions: These questions send the reader back to the text for more careful attention to the evidence presented there.

Research Projects: Readers are pointed toward areas of further inquiry connected to each chapter. Suggestions are provided for projects that encourage deeper research and analysis.

Series Glossary of Key Terms: This back-of-the book glossary contains terminology used throughout this series. Words found here increase the reader's ability to read and comprehend higher-level books and articles in this field.

GETTING ORIENTED WITH THE TERMS

Aggregate: combined score of matches between two teams in a two-match (with each often referred to as "legs") format, typically with each team playing one home match.

Away goals rule: tie-breaker applied in some competitions with two-legged matches. In cases where the aggregate score is tied, the team that has scored more goals away from home is deemed the winner.

Cap: each appearance by a player for his national team is referred to as a cap, a reference to an old English tradition where players would all receive actual caps.

Challenge: common term for a tackle—the method of a player winning the ball from an opponent—executed when either running at, beside, or sliding at the opponent.

Clean sheet: referencing no marks being made on the score sheet, when a goalkeeper or team does not concede a single goal during a match; a shutout.

Derby: match between two, usually local, rivals; e.g., Chelsea and Arsenal, both of which play in London.

Dummy: skill move performed by a player receiving a pass from a teammate; the player receiving the ball will intentionally allow the ball to run by them to a teammate close by without touching it, momentarily confusing the opponent as to who is playing the ball.

Equalizer: goal that makes the score even or tied.

First touch: refers to the initial play on a ball received by a player.

Football: a widely used name for soccer. Can also refer to the ball.

Group of death: group in a cup competition that is unusually competitive because the number of strong teams in the group is greater than the number of qualifying places available for the next phase of the tournament.

Kit: soccer-specific clothing worn by players, consisting at the minimum of a shirt, shorts, socks, specialized footwear, and (for goalkeepers) specialized gloves.

Loan: when a player temporarily plays for a club other than the one they are currently contracted to. Such a loan may last from a few weeks to one or more seasons.

Marking: defensive strategy that is either executed man-to-man or by zone, where each player is responsible for a specific area on the pitch.

Match: another word for game.

One touch: style of play in which the ball is passed around quickly using just one touch.

One-two: skill move in which Player One passes the ball to Player Two and runs past the opponent, whereupon they immediately receive the ball back from Player Two in one movement. Also known as a *give-and-go*.

Pitch: playing surface for a game of soccer; usually a specially prepared grass field. Referred to in the Laws of the Game as the field of play.

Set piece: dead ball routine that the attacking team has specifically practiced, such as a free kick taken close to the opposing goal, or a corner kick.

Through-ball: pass from the attacking team that goes straight through the opposition's defense to a teammate who runs to the ball.

Touch line: markings along the side of the pitch, indicating the boundaries of the playing area. Throw-ins are taken from behind this line.

Youth system (academy): young players are contracted to the club and trained to a high standard with the hope that some will develop into professional players. Some clubs provide academic as well as soccer education.

INTRODUCTION

For some countries, qualifying for the world's most popular sporting event is a foregone conclusion. Soccer fans in Germany, Brazil, and Italy can safely buy their tickets to watch their beloved teams play as soon as FIFA announces the location of the next World Cup. These countries have consistently produced players of quality and skill generation after generation, and are not only there at every World Cup, but usually threaten to win the tournament as well.

The case of Germany, Brazil, and Italy is the exception, however, because for most countries, getting into the World Cup final field is very difficult. Only 15 percent of the teams that try actually qualify every four years. For most national teams, qualification is a monumental achievement. When Denmark qualified for the 2002 World Cup in Japan and South Korea, the team's sponsor rewarded it with 1.1 million in Danish currency for the players. It was just the third time in its history that Denmark had qualified. When Saudi Arabia's team qualified for the first time in 1994, each player received a $25,000 bonus. Just getting in is a big deal.

Most countries have never qualified for the World Cup. Countries such as Angola, Canada, China, Congo, Cuba, Haiti, Indonesia, Iraq, Israel, Jamaica, Kuwait, Slovakia, Togo, Trinidad and Tobago, Ukraine, United Arab Emirates, and Wales have only qualified one time in their histories.

There are some big countries on that list. When it comes to getting into the World Cup, size is not everything. China has more than a billion people, but just one appearance. Uruguay, on the other hand, has fewer than four million people, but has five top-four finishes and two wins to show for 12 appearances. When soccer is the true passion of the nation, it is reflected in World Cup success.

Other lightly populated countries such as Paraguay, Switzerland, and the Netherlands all have excellent qualification records. Cameroon is an emerging African nation with seven World Cup appearances, the most of any team from that continent. Perhaps Cameroon star Roger Milla said it best when he simply stated the feeling behind the accomplishment, "Football allows a little country to become a big one."

CHAPTER 1

WORLD REGIONS

The world is a big place, and managing the hundreds of confederations affiliated with the world's most popular sport is a big job. That job falls to soccer's worldwide governing body, the Fédération Internationale de Football Association (FIFA). Based in Switzerland, FIFA has 211 member associations, the vast majority of which represent individual countries. FIFA recognizes regional confederations, which geographically group each country into one of six confederations that line up with the Earth's six populated continents.

In alphabetical order of the abbreviations by which they are commonly referred to, the confederations are: the Asian Football Confederation (AFC); the Confédération Africaine de Football (CAF); the Confederation of North, Central American, and Caribbean Association Football (CONCACAF); the Confederación Sudamericana de Fútbol (CONMEBOL); the Oceania Football Conference (OFC); and the Union of European Football Associations (UEFA). There are a few geographic **quirks**, most notably that Australia is an AFC member after leaving the OFC in 2006.

Japan, one of the best teams in the AFC, has qualified for every World Cup since 1998

AFC

The AFC was founded in the Philippines in 1954 with 12 member nations. There are now 47 nations represented in the AFC, which is headquartered in Kuala Lumpur, Malaysia.

Iran, Australia, and Japan have been the best teams in the AFC over the past decade. Japan has won a record four AFC Asian Cups, the confederation's top competition. In terms of World Cup success, Japan has qualified for each of the last five World Cup final tournaments, while

Japanese star Shinji Okazaki (L) has enjoyed a successful club career in Europe

South Korea has qualified for nine in a row. Since the AFC went from two to four qualifying spots in 1998, only South Korea and Japan have qualified for every tournament. Iran, Saudi Arabia, China, and Australia have also qualified in that time. In 2002, South Korea finished fourth, the best-ever result for an AFC team.

The AFC is not traditionally a confederation that **churns** out stars of the sport, but it produces some very good players. Omar Abdulrahman of the United Arab Emirates was named Asian Footballer of the Year for 2016. He plays in the UAE's top league.

Other players have branched out to play in the world's best leagues. Shinji Okazaki of Japan has been a striker in Europe's top leagues since 2011. After five seasons in the German Bundesliga with Stuttgart and Mainz, Okazaki moved to Leicester City in England's Premier League. For his country, Okazaki has scored more than 50 goals, including two in the World Cup.

South Korea's Son Heung-min is a midfielder for his country's team who followed a similar path to that of Okazaki. Son started at Hamburg in the Bundesliga at age 18, then played with Bayer Leverkusen before moving to Tottenham in the Premier League.

South Korea's Son Heung-min has played in both the Bundesliga and the Premier League

CAF

The confederation representing Africa was formed in 1954 with South Africa, Egypt, Sudan, and Ethiopia as representing members. This took place at the 29th FIFA Congress in Switzerland. Some countries argued that the standard of play in Africa was not good enough to be granted confederation status, but Africa's inclusion passed by a 24–17 vote. Today, the CAF has 56 member associations, including Egypt, seven-time winners of the Africa Cup of Nations, the confederation's top competition.

African nations have sent several strong teams to the World Cup over the years. Morocco was the first African team to get out of the group stage, advancing to the second round in 1986. Morocco has qualified for four World Cups. Other countries with at least that many appearances include Algeria, Cameroon, Nigeria, and Tunisia. Of these, only Tunisia has failed to advance past the group stage. The Indomitable Lions of Cameroon were quarterfinalists in 1990, the farthest an African team has ever advanced. Other nations to match this accomplishment include Senegal in 2002 and Ghana in 2010.

Pierre-Emerick Aubameyang plays for Gabon in the CAF and plays his club soccer in the Bundesliga

African nation players are well represented in the world's top leagues. Riyad Mahrez of Algeria was named African Footballer of the Year in 2016. The winger played seven seasons in France before moving to Premier League Club Leicester City in 2014.

Another standout African player is 2015 African Footballer of the Year Pierre-Emerick Aubameyang of Gabon. One of the best strikers in the world, Aubameyang also started his club career in France, playing five seasons there before signing with Borussia Dortmund in the Bundesliga. He scored more than 80 goals in his first four seasons in Germany.

FIFA CONFEDERATIONS

as of Sept 15, 2017

CONCACAF:

- Founded 1961
- 41 member associations
- Top teams –
  Mexico, USA, Costa Rica
- Most World Cup appearances –
  Mexico (15)
- Best World Cup Result –
  3rd (USA 1930)

CONMEBOL:

- Founded 1957
- 10 member associations
- Top teams –
  Brazil, Argentina, Uruguay, Colombia
- Most World Cup appearances –
  Brazil (21)
- Best World Cup Result –
  1st (Brazil 5, Argentina 2, Uruguay 2)

UEFA:

- Founded 1954
- 55 member associations
- Top teams – Germany, Italy, England, Spain, Portugal
- Most World Cup appearances – Germany & Italy (18)
- Best World Cup Result – 1st (Italy 4, Germany 4, England 1, France 1, Spain 1)

AFC:

- Founded 1954
- 47 member associations
- Top teams – Iran, Japan, Australia, South Korea, Saudi Arabia
- Most World Cup appearances – South Korea (10)
- Best World Cup Result – 4th (South Korea 2002)

CAF:

- Founded 1961
- 56 member associations
- Top teams – Egypt, Senegal, Cameroon, Nigeria, Tunisia
- Most World Cup appearances – Cameroon (7)
- Best World Cup Result – 7th (Cameroon 1990, Senegal 2002, Ghana 2010)

OFC:

- Founded 1966
- 14 member associations
- Top teams – New Zealand
- Most World Cup appearances – Australia & New Zealand (2)
- Best World Cup Result – 16th (Australia 2006)

Mexico has historically been the best team in CONCACAF, qualifying for the last six World Cups and advancing to the second round in each

CONCACAF

CONCACAF came out of the merger of two existing confederations in 1961: one of these represented Canada, Mexico, and the United States, while the other represented 10 Central American and Caribbean nations. The merger took place in Mexico City, but CONCACAF is now headquartered in Miami with 41 member associations.

Mexico is historically the best team in the confederation. It has won seven CONCACAF Gold Cups, the most of any country in the confederation. The United States has won five. Both countries have had moderate success at the World Cup level. Prior to 2018, Mexico had qualified for 15 World Cups, and the United States for 10.

No other CONCACAF country has been to more than four. Mexico has been to the quarterfinals twice, in 1970 and 1986. The United States went to the quarterfinals in 2002, and actually finished third in 1930. Costa Rica is the only other confederation country to make it as far as the quarterfinals, achieving this in 2014.

CONCACAF boasts several world-class players. Tim Howard of the United States is a three-time CONCACAF Goalkeeper of the Year. He had a 13-season run in the Premier League before returning home to play Major League Soccer in 2016.

Bryan Ruiz (in red) has earned more than 100 caps for Costa Rica

Most of the world's powerful soccer nations are big countries with sizeable populations. The advantage of this is the more people a country has, the more athletes there are to choose from to make up a national soccer team. There are exceptions on either side, however. China and India are two of the most populated countries on earth, but neither has ever had a good national soccer team as the sport is not one of focus for these countries. The most notable exception on the small side is Uruguay. This South American nation is soccer-mad, and has had great success despite having just more than three million people.

The least populated country to ever qualify for the World Cup is Iceland. The tiny island nation in the middle of the North Atlantic qualified out of UEFA for Russia 2018. With a population around 334,000, Iceland is four times smaller than the previous smallest country to qualify - Trinidad and Tobago in 2006. Iceland's success grows out of a soccer-mad culture. It has more than 20,000 registered players and more than 650 professional coaches.

2016 CONCACAF Player of the Year Bryan Ruiz of Costa Rica plays at Sporting CP in Portugal's Primeira Liga. He has more than 100 caps for his country. Fellow countryman Keylor Navas is the goalkeeper for international club power Real Madrid in Spain, where he has started since 2015. He has helped Los Blancos (a nickname for the club) to their first La Liga title in five seasons in 2017, plus back-to-back UEFA Champions League club championships in 2016 and 2017.

CONMEBOL

The confederation representing South America had its beginnings in 1916 in Argentina with three more founding members: Brazil, Chile, and Uruguay. Today, 10 of the continent's 13 countries are CONMEBOL members (the other three are with CONCACAF). The confederation is now headquartered in Paraguay.

Lionel Messi, one of the best players in the world, leads Argentina, one of the best teams in CONMEBOL

Brazil and Argentina are not only the best teams in CONMEBOL but are also two of the very best in the world. Between them the countries have seven World Cup titles, with Brazil claiming five. Brazil has 11 top-four results and Argentina has five. Uruguay also has five top-four finishes at the World Cup, including two titles. Uruguay won the first two World Cups but has only cracked the top four once since 1970. Of the other CONMEBOL nations, Colombia, Paraguay, and Peru have all been quarterfinalists, and Chile finished third in 1952.

CONMEBOL nations produce some of the very best players in the game. World superstar Lionel Messi is from Argentina. He is a five-time World Player of the Year. The striker was voted best player at the 2014 World Cup, where Argentina was runner-up to Germany.

Brazilian phenomenon Neymar da Silva Santos Júnior (better known simply as Neymar) is the best player for his country, and is one of the top forwards in the entire world. Neymar has more than 50 goals for Brazil since 2010. He was named to the FIFA World Cup Dream Team for the 2014 tournament, and was also voted best player at the 2013 FIFA Confederations Cup.

Neymar stars for soccer powerhouse Brazil, winner of five World Cups

Other standout South American players include Alexis Sánchez of Chile, Sergio Agüero of Argentina, and Luis Suárez of Uruguay.

Australia left the OFC in search of better competition in 2006

OFC

The OFC, which includes the islands of the South Pacific, lost one of its founding members in 2006 when Australia joined the AFC. Since the confederation's **inception** in 1966, Australia was by far the biggest and best member nation. Australia has won World Cup qualifiers in the OFC region by scores of 31–0 and 22–0. As a consequence, this lack of competition was not preparing Australia well for play against better teams at the World Cup level. With their switch to the Asian confederation, Australia plays better competition, and the remaining 14 OFC members have a chance to qualify to play in the World Cup. The OFC is headquartered in New Zealand.

New Zealand has been the best team in the confederation since Australia's departure. The OFC does not have a guaranteed spot for which it can qualify a team in the World Cup. Therefore, New Zealand is the only current OFC team that has ever qualified for a World Cup, doing so in both 1982 and 2010. The team failed to win a match on either occasion.

Ryan Thomas of New Zealand is one of the OFC's top players. Thomas is a winger who plays for PEC Zwolle in the Dutch Eredivisie. He was voted OFC Footballer of the Year in 2015.

Thomas' fellow countryman Chris Wood has also had a successful European club career. Wood is a forward who has played nine seasons in England, mostly in the English Football League Championship, the country's second-tier league. He most recently played at Leeds United, where he scored 40 goals in 80 matches in his first two seasons.

UEFA

Europe's confederation is the world's most powerful and most competitive. UEFA has 55 member nations, beginning with 25 founding members in 1954 in Switzerland, where it is still based.

UEFA has several powerful member countries as Europe produces the vast majority of the world's top players. Germany is a four-time World Cup winner, as is Italy. Spain, France,

Portugal's Cristiano Ronaldo has been voted best player in the world five times

and England have also won the World Cup. Dozens of other member countries have qualified and done extremely well. The Czech Republic, for example, is a two-time runner-up, in 1934 and 1962. The Netherlands has been runner-up three times. Besides the winners, at least eight other UEFA countries have finished in the top four at a World Cup.

Cristiano Ronaldo of Portugal is one of UEFA's and the world's top players, as demonstrated in this highlight reel

The list of UEFA's top players starts with five-time World Player of the Year Cristiano Ronaldo of Portugal. The sensational forward has scored more than 75 goals in more than 140 appearances for Portugal since 2003. He led Portugal to the Euro 2016 championship. On the club level, his teams have won five league championships, four European club championships, and two club World Cups.

Other European greats include: Antoine Griezmann, N'Golo Kanté, and Paul Pogba of France; Andrés Iniesta, David De Gea, and Sergio Ramos of Spain; Manuel Neuer and Toni Kroos of Germany; Harry Kane of England; and Gareth Bale of Wales.

Toni Kroos (L) of Germany is one of the best midfielders in Europe and the world

TEXT-DEPENDENT QUESTIONS:

1. How many member associations does FIFA have?

2. How many times did American Tim Howard win CONCACAF Goalkeeper of the Year?

3. How many times has the Netherlands been runner-up at the World Cup?

 RESEARCH PROJECT:

Only countries from UEFA or CONMEBOL have ever won the World Cup. Do some research on the other four confederations to determine which countries are the best in their regions. Write an opinion that outlines your logic in describing which of these other regions will be the first to produce a World Cup winner.

Fédération Internationale
de Football Association

WORDS TO UNDERSTAND:

aggregate: the whole sum or amount

recourse: an opportunity or choice to use or do something in order to deal with a problem or situation

revoked: to officially cancel the power or effect of something (such as a law, license, agreement, etc.); to make something not valid

CHAPTER 2

QUALIFYING FOR THE WORLD CUP

With its 211 member nations, FIFA's task every four years is to narrow this field down to the 32 that will qualify to play in the World Cup tournament. This is a process that begins about eight months after the final match of the previous World Cup is played. Qualifying for the World Cup is done within each confederation.

Of the 32 spots, only 31 are available for qualification. One spot goes to the host nation. This practice started for the third World Cup in 1938.

Before 2006, the defending champion also received an automatic bid. However, after defending champion and top-ranked France failed to win a match or score a goal in the group stage in 2002—leading to its early elimination from the competition—the champion's privilege was **revoked**.

Of the 31 spots that are contested, 29 of them are assigned to the various confederations as follows:

UEFA: 13 spots   **CONMEBOL: 4 spots**   **CONCACAF: 3 spots**

CAF: 5 spots   **AFC: 4 spots**   **OFC: no guaranteed spot**

The two remaining spots are decided by a playoff involving four confederations. A draw decides whether a CONMEBOL team will play a team from the AFC or the OFC for one spot. The team from the confederation that is not drawn (AFC or OFC) then plays a CONCACAF team for the second spot.

AFC Qualifying

Asian qualifying is the first to get underway in the current qualification format. For the 2018 World Cup, for example, AFC qualifying matches started in March of 2015. The 12 countries in the confederation that are ranked lowest by FIFA play a series of what are called two-legged ties. This means that the countries are paired into six matchups, and within each matchup the teams play a home-and-away series, meaning they play one match in country A and the other in country B. If both games are draws, or each team wins, then **aggregate** goals are used as a tiebreaker, with away goals given more weight.

The six winners are then included with the remaining 34 AFC teams, and all are put into a draw for eight groups of five teams. This round-robin for the second-round group stage takes about nine months to play, and the one for 2018 wrapped up in March of 2016. The eight group winners advance along with the four group runners-up with the most points.

These 12 countries are then drawn into two groups of six for a third round. The top-two teams in each group after a round-robin qualify for the World Cup. The teams that finish third in each group then play each other for the right to advance to an interconfederation playoff against a team from CONCACAF for a qualifying spot.

Tristan Do (L) of Thailand in action during the FIFA World Cup-qualifying match between Thailand and Chinese Taipei on November 12, 2015, at Rajamangala Stadium in Thailand

Since the 1986 World Cup, interconfederation playoff matches have been used to determine which confederations get the last spot or two in the final tournament. That 1986 World Cup is the only one in which a UEFA team was forced into a playoff for a spot. The OFC does not have a guaranteed spot and sends a team to a playoff every four years. The playoffs are conducted as home-and-away ties. Beginning with the 2006 World Cup, two playoff ties are contested, with two spots up for grabs. Here are the records of each confederation that has competed in a playoff for World Cup qualification from 1986–2014.

UEFA	1–0
CONMEBOL	4–1
CONCACAF	2–1
OFC	4–6
AFC	1–4

CONCACAF Qualifying

The first round of CONCACAF qualifying works the same as it does in the AFC: here the 14 lowest FIFA-ranked teams play seven two-legged ties. The seven winners then advance to the second round. In CONCACAF, however, the second round is not a group stage.

In the second round, the seven first-round winners are combined with the next 13 lowest-ranked teams. The 20 teams then play 10 more two-legged ties, yielding 10 winners.

The third round then combines the 10 winners with the next two lowest teams in FIFA's rankings, and the 12 teams play six more two-legged ties. The six round-three winners then join FIFA's six highest-ranked teams in a fourth-round group stage.

Mexico's fans are passionately loyal to El Tricolor (or El Tri), the nickname for their national team

The 12 teams are drawn into three groups of four. Each team then plays six home-and-away matches (one set with each group member). The top two nations from each group advance to the final group stage.

The six teams then each play a home-and-away set against the other group members. The top three in the group after all matches have been played qualify for the World Cup. The fourth-place team qualifies for a playoff match against a team from the AFC for the 30th World Cup spot.

OFC Qualifying

The OFC does not have a separate World Cup qualifying process. It uses the results of its own confederation tournaments to determine the team that will play for a chance to get into the World Cup. As the smallest and least-experienced confederation, the OFC is not guaranteed a spot. One team from the confederation plays

The Solomon Islands played in the final round of OFC qualifying to get into a playoff for a spot in the 2018 World Cup

its way into an interconfederation playoff match against a South American team for a chance to be included in the final tournament.

For Russia 2018, it started with a league tournament between four countries: American Samoa, the Cook Islands, Samoa, and Tonga. Samoa won that tournament, which qualified it for the 2016 OFC Nations Cup. The teams were drawn into two groups of four, with the top three teams in each group advancing after a round-robin within the group. In the third round, there are two groups of three teams drawn, with each team playing four matches in home-and-away sets against other group members. The two group winners then advance to a fourth-round playoff tie against each other. The winner of the tie goes to the two-legged interconfederation playoff against a CONMEBOL team.

CONMEBOL Qualifying

Watch club teammates Neymar and Luis Suarez battle as captains for opposing teams in a 2018 CONMEBOL World Cup qualifying match in Brazil

Qualifying in South America is quite different than in other confederations as CONMEBOL only has 10 member nations. There are no groups and no rounds. All 10 teams compete together to play a home-and-away set against every other team. There is one set of standings (or a single table, as it is often called), and the four teams that end up at the top of the table after each one has played 18 matches automatically qualify for the World Cup.

The rest of the teams are eliminated except for the fifth-place team, which is given the chance to qualify through another route. That team

Brazil was the first team to qualify for the 2018 World Cup

plays a two-legged playoff tie against the winner of the OFC to determine the 31st spot in the World Cup.

For Russia 2018, Brazil was the first team to qualify for one of the 31 available spots. With a 3–0 win over Paraguay in March of 2017, the Brazilians reached their 10th win and had already accumulated enough points to guarantee they could finish no lower than fourth in CONMEBOL qualifying.

CAF Qualifying

Qualifying in Africa is similar to that in Asia and CONCACAF. Based on how teams are ranked by FIFA at the beginning of qualifying, the 26 lowest teams in the rankings are paired up to play two-legged ties in the first round. This produces 13 winners to advance to round two.

In the second round, the 27 teams at the top of FIFA's CAF rankings join the 13 winners, and those 40 teams are again paired off to play two-legged ties. This produces 20 winners to advance to round three.

The third round is a group stage, with the 20 remaining teams drawn into five groups of four. The teams then play home-and-away sets

Nigeria's soccer team hopes to repeat its prior World Cup successes in 2018. Nigeria has qualified for five of the last six World Cups and advanced past the first round three times

against each team in their group. The draw is critical as there is no **recourse** after this round. Only the five group winners qualify for spots in the World Cup. If two strong teams end up in the same group, it is guaranteed that one will not qualify.

For Russia 2018, for example, both Egypt and Congo drew into Group E. They were ranked first and third in the CAF by FIFA. Also, Cameroon, Nigeria, and Algeria all drew into group B. Of the 20 teams, those three ranked 5th, 6th, and 8th in the CAF, respectively.

UEFA

For European qualifying, teams qualify for the World Cup in two stages. For the first round, the 54 eligible teams are drawn into nine groups of six. Each team plays a home-and-away set against each of its other group members. After 10 matches, the winners of each group automatically qualify for the World Cup.

Robert Lewandowski of Poland (L) attacks against Romania in a World Cup 2018-qualifying match in June 2017

That means nine teams qualify after the first round. There are then four spots left to be determined out of this confederation. For the second round, the eight non-group-winning teams that have the best record in the first round are eligible, regardless of group or group placement. Those eight teams are then paired to play home-and-away ties to determine the last four qualifying spots.

Viktor Kovalenko of Ukraine (in yellow) fights
for a ball against Iceland defenders during a FIFA World Cup
2018-qualifying match in September 2016

TEXT-DEPENDENT QUESTIONS:

1. When did the host nation begin getting an automatic qualification for the World Cup?
2. How many teams are involved in the fourth round of World Cup qualifying in the CONCACAF confederation?
3. How many teams are eligible for World Cup qualifying from the UEFA confederation?

RESEARCH PROJECT:

Compare and contrast the qualifying methods employed by each confederation. Describe which confederation has the best qualification format and explain why you feel that way.

WORDS TO UNDERSTAND:

bona-fide: real or genuine

caliber: level of excellence, skill, etc.

daunting: tending to make people afraid or less confident; very difficult to do or deal with

respectively: separately or individually

DRAW TO THE DEATH

Soccer is a game of strategy, execution, teamwork, and skill. Good use of all of these elements will maximize a team's chance to win. In World Cup tournament play, however, there is another element that can play a large part in a team's chances of advancing in the tournament: the draw.

Going to Pots

In the World Cup, the 32 teams that qualify to play for the sport's greatest championship are the best their countries have to offer. This does not mean, however, that all teams are of the same **caliber**. Some countries, especially those from Europe and South America, are more skilled than others. FIFA takes this into account when putting the World Cup final tournament together. Before the draw to determine which teams will be grouped together, teams are assigned to pots based on their FIFA ranking. A pot is a grouping of eight teams, and the tournament groups are drawn from these pots.

Group Dynamic

FIFA ranks all of the teams from its member nations based on match results. The first pot is determined based on these rankings at the time of the draw, which is usually held about eight months before the tournament. This pot is the seeded pot. It consists of the top seven teams in the rankings, plus the host nation. The other three pots are then assembled based on geography, where the aim is to keep countries from the same confederation together where possible. Since the eight tournament groups of four are drawn by selecting one team from each pot, all the teams from the seeded pot will be in different groups. This ensures that the very best teams in the world will not face the possibility of eliminating each other in the group stage.

All Together Now

When the eight groups are drawn, each is guaranteed to contain one of the top seven teams in the world or the host nation. After that, the hope is that each group will have no more than one team from most of the world's six confederations, but that is all in the luck of the draw. In 2014, for example, the confederations were represented like this for the World Cup in Brazil: **AFC – 4; CAF – 5; CONCACAF – 4; CONMEBOL – 6; OFC – 0; UEFA – 13.** Since the top seven teams and the hosts all came from two confederations, the pots looked like this:

Pot 1 (Seeded): CONMEBOL – 4, UEFA – 4

Pot 2 (CAF and CONMEBOL): CAF – 5, CONMEBOL – 2

Pot 3 (AFC and CONCACAF): AFC – 4, CONCACAF – 4

Pot 4 (UEFA): 9

Odd Man Out

Because UEFA qualifies 13 teams, Pot 4 had an extra team and Pot 2 had one less. Traditionally, the team that moves out of Pot 4 was determined by FIFA ranking: the lowest-ranked team was the one that would move. For the 2014 draw, however, that changed. A draw was held to determine which UEFA team would move out instead, and Italy moved from Pot 4 to Pot 2. This change was controversial because it was proposed and backed by two French officials: the FIFA secretary general and the UEFA president, **respectively**. France was the lowest-ranked team and would have moved out under the old selection method.

CONMEBOL teams like Chile battle for up to five qualifying spots at the World Cup

Under the current 32 team format, five World Cup groups will always include two UEFA teams like Hungary and Sweden

Separation Anxiety

With the pots determined, the drawing of the tournament groupings can begin. In order to ensure geographic separation where possible, however, the UEFA and CONMEBOL teams in the seeded pot are first split into sub-pots based on confederation. In 2014, one CONMEBOL team was drawn and automatically grouped with Italy from Pot 2. With only teams from Pots 3 and 4 remaining for selection to that group, this ensured that no group would have more than two UEFA teams. Since UEFA qualifies 13 teams, five groups will have two UEFA teams.

The draw then continues by assigning each of the Pot 1 teams to be the lead team for each group (A through H), with the host automatically assigned to Group A. Group A then draws its teams in order from Pot 2, then Pot 3, then Pot 4. Then Group B is filled in, then group C, and so on, through Group H. The only deviation from this occurs when a group headed by a CONMEBOL team is selecting when CONMEBOL teams are still not chosen in Pot 2.

In the case of 2014, Brazil was the host and therefore assigned from Pot 1 as the lead team in Group A. However, as Pot 2 contained two CONMEBOL teams, Group A could not be selected until both of the CONMEBOL teams had been chosen from Pot 2. That meant Group B, with Spain as the lead team, was filled in before Group A.

When all was said and done, Groups B, D, E, G, and H had two UEFA teams each. Each group had no more than one team from each of the other confederations.

Group of Death

The Mexican media at the 1970 World Cup in Mexico coined the morbid-sounding term "group of death." The term was used to describe Group 3 going into the tournament (at the time, numbers, not letters, designated the groups). The group contained England, Brazil, Czechoslovakia, and Romania, and was considered by experts to be highly competitive. The English were the defending World Cup champions, and featured stars like Bobby Moore, Bobby Charlton, and Gordon Banks. The Brazilians, who ultimately won the tournament, were considered by most experts to be the best team in the world, with superstar Pelé, Carlos Alberto, and Jairzinho. Romania featured one of the country's all-time greats in Nicolae Dobrin and Czechoslovakia was just one World Cup removed from its 1962 runner-up performance.

The Mexican press revived the term in 1982 for the World Cup in Italy. This time, it was applied to Group C, which featured three previous champions: three-time winners Brazil, defending champions Argentina, and two-time winners and hosts Italy (which would go on to win that year for its third title).

At the 1998 World Cup, Tunisia rounded out the group of death as the 19th-ranked team in the world

By the 1986 tournament, which like 1970's was also in Mexico, the term was popular with the English-language media as well and was used to describe Group E, where UEFA teams Scotland and Denmark joined former champions West Germany and Uruguay. This was the first time the champion did not come from the group of death—but it was close, as Argentina won by beating West Germany 3–2 in the final.

Goal! A soccer fan cheers during the final match between France and Italy in FIFA World Cup 2006. Italy won the tournament after winning the group of death in round one

Today, the term is commonly used in group-format tournaments, and the media quickly anoints one of the groups as the "group of death," whether the group is overly tough or not. In modern usage, it refers to the most competitive group, but not necessarily the most **daunting** one.

Defining Death

There is no common standard for a "group of death." Do all teams in the group need to be great, or will having three great teams qualify as "death"-worthy? This is just one of the possible undefined qualification criteria. Jonathan Liew, a journalist at the London-based *Daily Telegraph*, devised a formula based on the FIFA world rankings to determine the toughest groups at every World Cup since 1994, the first tournament since FIFA started its rankings.

 ## SIDEBAR: GROUP OF LIFE

Not every group in a World Cup draw will be a "group of death." In fact, some are so far from being difficult, they are facetiously referred to as a "group of life." Take Group H from the 2002 World Cup, for example. The teams and their world rankings were:

Belgium (23)	**Russia (28)**
Tunisia (31)	**Japan (32)**

Without a single top-20 team, this was not a challenging group, but it was competitive. That is not always the case in these groups. In 2006, the "group of life" was Group B:

England (10)	**Sweden (16)**
Paraguay (33)	**Trinidad and Tobago (47)**

England and Sweden barely broke a sweat, with both going undefeated in advancing to the next round. They played their third matches against each other knowing they had both already advanced. That match ended in a draw.

Defender Jorge Fucile
of Uruguay (R) battles
Phil Jagielka of England late
in Uruguay's group of death
win at the 2014 World Cup

Death Watch

According to Liew's calculations, only one World Cup, the 2010 event, did not have a really tough group. The other five all had a group of death. In 1994 it was Group E, with three-time champions Italy, plus Norway, Ireland, and Mexico. In 1998, the media was quick to assign the death mantle to Group D, with Spain, Nigeria, Paraguay, and Bulgaria. While Spain was ranked third, the next-best team was Paraguay at only 29th, and Nigeria had the lowest ranking in the entire tournament. The true group of death in 1998 was Group G—the toughest group since the rankings began, according to the formula. On first glance, the group with Romania, England, Colombia, and Tunisia did not look that difficult. The Romanians, English, and Colombians, however, were all ranked between fourth and eighth in the world. Tunisia was the weakest team in the group, but it was still 19th-best in the world. With four teams in the top 20, this is the toughest group in modern World Cup history, from which England and Romania survived.

Watch the highlights of the match between 1998 World Cup group of death survivors England and Romania

In 2002, the clear group of death was Group F. With former champions England and Argentina, plus Sweden and Nigeria, the teams were all very good. No team in the group had more than one win in group play, and England and Sweden advanced. In 2006, the media dubbed Group C, with Argentina, the Netherlands, Ivory Coast, and Serbia and Montenegro as the group of death. By Liew's formula, however, it was too easy a group to qualify as such, with first-timers Ivory Coast and

Thomas Müller (#13) of Germany controls the ball during the World Cup final match between Argentina and Germany. Germany won the tournament after winning a group of death

Serbia and Montenegro. But Group F was a **bona-fide** group of death. The Czech Republic, USA, Italy, and Ghana were a much tougher group. Eventual champions Italy and Ghana advanced.

In 2010, the media declared Group G to be the group of death. With Brazil, Portugal, Ivory Coast, and North Korea, it appeared pretty good. Yet a proper look requires an examination of the North Korean side. By far the worst in the tournament, North Korea offered almost no opposition, losing all three group matches and scoring only one goal. The formula does not allow for a group with a team that weak to qualify as a true group of death.

So far, the 2014 World Cup in Brazil is the only tournament to have two groups qualify as a group of death by Liew's formula. The first, and also the one anointed as such by the media, was Group G, with three-time champions Germany, the USA, Portugal (featuring World Player of the Year Cristiano Ronaldo), and Ghana. Eventual winners Germany and the USA advanced. The tougher group, however, was Group D, with former champions Uruguay, Italy, and England, as well as Costa Rica. Uruguay and Costa Rica advanced from what is the third-toughest group in modern World Cup history.

TEXT-DEPENDENT QUESTIONS:

1. Under the current World Cup group selection system, how many teams are included in a pot?
2. How many groups at the World Cup will typically contain UEFA teams?
3. Which groups qualified as a group of death at the 2014 World Cup?

RESEARCH PROJECT:

Do some research on the groups of death described in this chapter. Choose the one you felt was the most difficult and explain your reasoning.

WORDS TO UNDERSTAND:

abstract: relating to, or involving, general ideas or qualities rather than specific people, objects, or actions

accredited: having official authorization or approval

dynamic: always active, energetic, or changing

CHAPTER 4

WORLD CUP AWARDS

Every four years, the World Cup tournament brings together soccer's brightest stars for a showcase of the sport watched by millions. Fueled by natural skill and national pride, some of these players rise to the challenge of the moment and perform at a level that singles them out as the best of the best. FIFA recognizes these players throughout and at the conclusion of every World Cup.

Man of the Match

The Man of the Match is an award given at the end of every World Cup match to the best player voted to have performed the best in the match. The award was first established in 2002. The vote is public, conducted via online poll on the FIFA website and social media platforms. Although the player winning the vote is typically from the winning side, this is not a rule of the process. Players from the losing side have occasionally been selected.

In 2014, Argentina's Lionel Messi led the tournament when he was named Man of the Match four times. Messi has been Man of the Match at the World Cup a record five times in his career. Arjen Robben of the Netherlands has also won five times. Wesley Snejder of the Netherlands also won four Man of the Match awards in a single World Cup, in 2010.

Argentina's Lionel Messi has been Man of the Match at the World Cup a record five times in his career, including four times at Brazil 2014

BEST
OF THE BEST

as of Sept 15, 2017

BRAZIL

PELÉ

BEST PLAYER,
1970 WORLD CUP

Total World Cups – 4
Total World Cup Goals – 12
Best World Cup Result – 1st (1958, 1962, 1970)

BRAZIL

RONALDO

BEST PLAYER,
1998 WORLD CUP

Total World Cups – 3
Total World Cup Goals – 15
Best World Cup Result – 1st (2002)

DIEGO MARADONA

BEST PLAYER, 1986 WORLD CUP

Total World Cups – 4
Total World Cup Goals – 8
Best World Cup Result – 1st (1986)

FRANCE

ZINEDINE ZIDANE

BEST PLAYER, 2006 WORLD CUP

Total World Cups – 3
Total World Cup Goals – 5
Best World Cup Result – 1st (1998)

ARGENTINA

LIONEL MESSI

BEST PLAYER, 2014 WORLD CUP

Total World Cups – 3
Total World Cup Goals – 5
Best World Cup Result – 2nd (2014)

SIDEBAR: GOLDEN BALLERS

Here are the players named as best of each World Cup since 1958. FIFA did not actually start awarding a trophy for the honor until 1982.

WORLD CUP	PLAYER	COUNTRY
Sweden 1958	Didi	Brazil
Chile 1962	Garrincha	Brazil
England 1966	Bobby Charlton	England
Mexico 1970	Pelé	Brazil
West Germany 1974	Johan Cruyff	Netherlands
Argentina 1978	Mario Kempes	Argentina
Spain 1982	Paolo Rossi	Italy
Mexico 1986	Diego Maradona	Argentina
Italy 1990	Salvatore Schillaci	Italy
USA 1994	Romário	Brazil
France 1998	Ronaldo	Brazil
Korea/Japan 2002	Oliver Kahn	Germany
Germany 2006	Zinedine Zidane	France
South Africa 2010	Diego Forlán	Uruguay
Brazil 2014	Lionel Messi	Argentina

Golden Ball

The Golden Ball is the name given to the World Cup player of the tournament. It was first awarded at the 1982 World Cup in Italy. It is awarded at the conclusion of the event to the player determined to be the best overall player of the tournament. The winner fittingly receives a golden trophy in the shape of a soccer ball. **Accredited** media representatives select the winner from a short list compiled by a FIFA technical committee. The Silver Ball and Bronze Ball go to the players that finish second and third in the voting, respectively.

Between 1958 and 1982, the award was simply called the Player of the Tournament, and no trophy was awarded. Since Brazil has won the most World Cup titles with five, it is no surprise that the country has produced the most winners of this award. Five Brazilians—from Didi in 1958 to Ronaldo in 1998—have been winners. Argentina has had three winners, despite only two titles. The team that may have the most surprising total is Germany, with just a single win by goalkeeper Oliver Kahn in 2002 despite four championships. Kahn is the only goalkeeper to ever win the award.

Winning the Golden Ball is not all about scoring goals. In fact, only twice in the Golden Ball era has the winner also been the highest goal scorer. Both times the players were Italians: Paolo Rossi in 1982 and Salvatore Schillaci in 1990.

The winner is also not always from the champion team. On seven occasions since 1958, the Golden Ball winner has played for a team that lost, including every World Cup after 1994.

Golden Boot

Formerly known as the Golden Shoe, the Golden Boot award involves no vote. It simply goes to the player who scores the most goals in the course of the World Cup tournament. The award was called the Golden Shoe from 1982 to 2006. Prior to 1982, statistics were kept on goal scoring, but no award was given for the most goals.

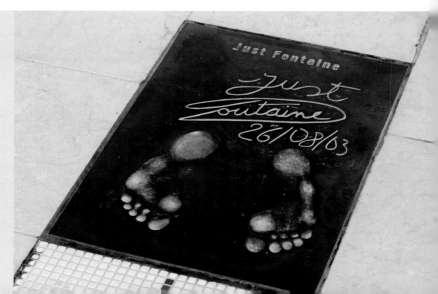

Only one player per year is immortalized on Monaco's Champion's Promenade. In 2003 it was French superstar Just Fontaine, who won the Golden Boot in 1958 with 13 goals at the World Cup

One of those times when no award was given was at the 1958 World Cup in Sweden. That was a tournament dominated by Brazil, led by a young Pelé to its first World Cup title. In the semifinals, Brazil faced France and won easily 5–2 behind a spectacular hat trick performance from Pelé. For the French, striker Just Fontaine scored the first goal for his team in that match. That goal was Fontaine's 13th goal of the tournament, a record that still stands today.

Colombian star James Rodríguez won the Golden Boot at the 2014 World Cup in Brazil

In the Golden Shoe era, Brazilian superstar Ronaldo set the standard with eight goals in the 2002 World Cup in South Korea and Japan. Brazil won the tournament for its fifth title as Ronaldo scored both goals in the final match for a 2–0 win against Germany.

After the award became the Golden Boot in 2010, young James Rodríguez of Colombia had the tournament of his professional career in Brazil in 2014. In Colombia's run to the quarterfinals, Rodríguez scored six times in five matches to win the award.

Golden Glove

The Golden Glove award is presented to the player determined to be the best goalkeeper in the tournament. The officials in the FIFA Technical Study Group decide on the award at the conclusion of the tournament.

Prior to 2010, the award was called the Lev Yashin Award after the star goalkeeper for the Soviet Union. Yashin played 74 matches for his national team from 1954 to 1967. He is the only goalkeeper to ever win

Spanish goalkeeper Iker Casillas won the Golden Glove at the 2010 World Cup after allowing a record low two goals in the tournament

the award given to the best player in Europe (the Ballon D'Or), and he is considered to be the model for the way modern goalkeepers play the position. The award was established following his death in 1990, and it was first given to Michel Preud'homme of Belgium in 1994.

Before the establishment of the Lev Yashin Award in 1994, there was no individual award for goalkeepers. They were, and still are, eligible to win the Golden Ball. Only Oliver Kahn has ever won both. Prior to 1994, the best goalkeeper in the tournament was considered to be the one selected to the post-tournament All-Star Team. Panels of experts and/or journalists at each World Cup choose this team.

Some players have won this award more quietly than others. Performances that stood out include Kahn's in 2002, who won despite losing the final to Brazil 2–0. Prior to that match, he had only given up three goals in six matches. In 2010, Spain's Iker Casillas led his team to victory as captain. Casillas only gave up two goals in the entire tournament, keeping five clean sheets, including a 1–0 win in the final.

Best Young Player

Players in the World Cup who were under 21 years old on January 1st of the year of the tournament are eligible for the Best Young Player award. The award was first given to Germany's Lucas Podolski, who scored three times in front of his home-country fans at the 2006 World Cup. Subsequent winners were Thomas Müller of Germany at the 2010 tournament in South Africa and Paul Pogba of France in Brazil in 2014.

To assess World Cups from 1958 to 2002, FIFA set up an online vote with the help of its Technical Study Group to let users choose the best young player from these past tournaments. The easiest choice for users was for the 1958 tournament, where they chose 17-year-old Pelé, who led Brazil to its first World Cup title that year. Users also chose the great Franz Beckenbauer, who was 20 years old at the 1966 World Cup in England. Der Kaiser, as the **dynamic** defender was known, scored a total of four goals in his very first World Cup tournament. England's Michael Owen made his World Cup debut in France at age 18. At that 1998 World Cup, Owen scored twice for his country in the tournament. American Landon Donovan is the only US player to have been selected for this award. At the 2002 World Cup in South Korea and Japan, Donovan scored two goals to help his team reach the quarterfinals.

Watch the teenage brilliance of England's Michael Owen at the 1998 World Cup

FIFA Fair Play Trophy

FIFA also awards a team trophy in addition to the one that goes to the champion. The FIFA Fair Play Trophy has been awarded since 1970 to the team that is judged to have the best record of playing fairly in the World Cup. Only teams that advance beyond the second round are eligible for this award.

This award has also evolved over the years. For the first three World Cups at which it was awarded, a paper certificate was given. The award then took the form of a gold trophy shaped like a cartoon character playing soccer named Sport Billy. This was the case from 1982 to 1990.

Since 1994, Sport Billy has been replaced on the trophy with a more **abstract** and artistic soccer-playing figure. Teams are generally judged to have played fairly if they receive fewer yellow or red cards throughout the course of the tournament. In 1970, the first-ever winners from Peru received no cards at all.

Dream Team

From 1930 to 2006, FIFA named a post-World Cup All-Star Team after each tournament that was chosen by various means until 1994, when it was selected by the FIFA Technical Study Group. Beginning with the 2010 tournament in South Africa, the All-Star Team was discontinued and replaced by what is now known as the Dream Team.

Teams that receive the fewest yellow or red cards during World Cup tournaments win the FIFA Fair Play Trophy

The Dream Team consists of an 11-player squad selected by online voting at FIFA.com following the World Cup. Voters select one goalkeeper, four defenders, six midfielders or forwards, and a manager. In both 2010 and 2014, voters selected the Golden Ball winner to the Dream Team. Golden Boot winner James Rodríguez was also selected in 2014, but Golden Boot winner Thomas Müller was left off the squad in 2010. In 2010, Spain had a player selected at every position, as did Germany in 2014. Each of these countries was the World Cup champion in those years.

Despite winning the Golden Boot, Germany's Thomas Müller was not chosen for the World Cup Dream Team in 2010

As evidenced by the changes to these awards over the years, FIFA is not afraid to make adjustments to keep the awards fresh and to engage fans by letting their voices be heard. That philosophy of change will expand to the tournament format itself in the not too distant future.

1. When was the Man of the Match award established at the World Cup?
2. How many goals did Ronaldo score at the 2002 World Cup?
3. Which Golden Boot winner was left off the Dream Team following the 2010 World Cup?

RESEARCH PROJECT:

Look up all the players who have been named best player at the World Cup. Research their statistics and any descriptions you can find of their play. Write a report on the player who you feel most deserved the award, and the player who you think was least deserving. Explain who you would have given the award to instead.

WORDS TO UNDERSTAND:

clamoring: a loud or strong demand for something by many people

emerging: newly created or noticed and growing in strength or popularity; becoming widely known or established

showcase: an event, occasion, etc., that shows the abilities or good qualities of someone or something in an attractive or favorable way

EXPANDING THE WORLD CUP

The World Cup has changed format several times since it debuted in 1930. That initial tournament, which used a round-robin group-play format for the first round, was by invitation only. It was open to a select few members of FIFA, and even then, the Association had to twist arms to get teams to travel all the way to Uruguay to play in the event, which was eventually won by the home team. Things have come a long way since then.

The Tournament Grows

By 1934, 36 countries were **clamoring** to be included in the World Cup so the tournament expanded to 16 teams and added qualification to set the field, including for the host nation (and eventual champion) Italy. The group-play format used in Uruguay was replaced by a single-match elimination setup.

Automatic qualification was granted to both the hosts and defending champions for the first time for France in 1938. The format was once again single-game elimination among the 16 qualified teams. Italy repeated as champions.

It took until 1950 for the world to be at peace again and for people to go back to playing soccer after the devastation of World War II. Due to the slow recovery in many countries following the war, only 13 teams participated in the 1950 World Cup, held in Brazil. The format was changed to a round-robin group-play format for each of two rounds, with four teams advancing to the final second round. Uruguay won its second title that year.

For 1954 in Switzerland, the World Cup was back up to 16 qualifying teams. Group play was used as the first-round format, but the round-robin was abandoned. Instead, within each four-team group, two seeded teams played each of two unseeded teams. Then the four group winners

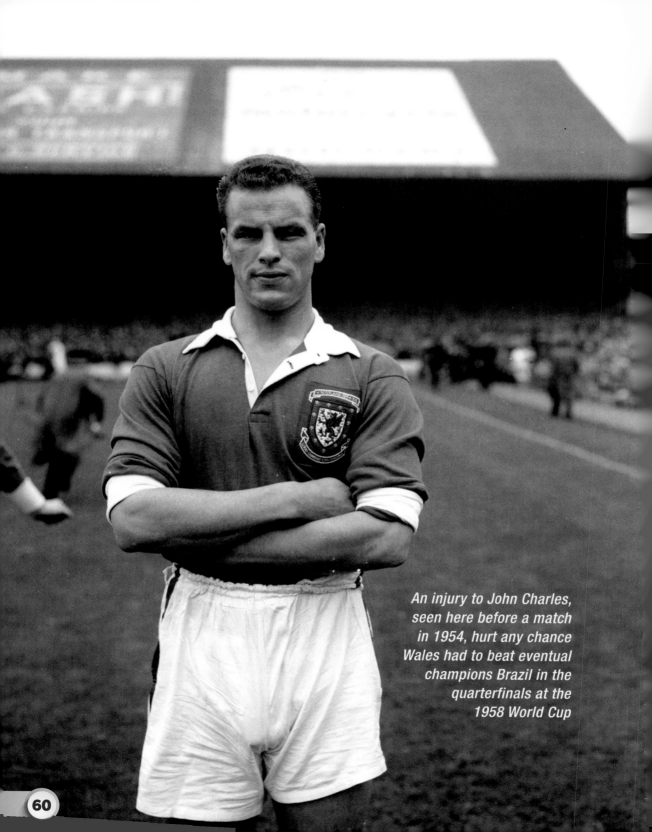

An injury to John Charles, seen here before a match in 1954, hurt any chance Wales had to beat eventual champions Brazil in the quarterfinals at the 1958 World Cup

played a two-round knockout stage to produce a finalist, while the two group runners-up did the same. West Germany came out of the runner-up bracket to upset Hungary 3–2.

In 1958, Sweden hosted the World Cup, and this time the 16 teams played a four-group round-robin, with the top two teams in each group advancing to a quarterfinal knockout stage. Brazil beat the host nation in the final for its first title.

From 1962 to 1970, the same format as in 1958 was used. In 1974 in West Germany, however, the eight teams that advanced from the opening-stage round-robin played another group stage in round two, which was also a round-robin. The home team won its second World Cup.

The 1978 event used the same format as in 1974. In 1982, however, came the first major expansion of the tournament, as the World Cup field increased to 24 teams. The World Cup in Spain opened more spots due to the need to include more teams from regions outside Europe. In prior events, Europe had taken 11 of the 14 available spots (the host and defending champions already had two of the 16 total). The three remaining spots went to the Americas (2) and Asia (1). In Spain, eight new spots were added, including three more for the Americas, two each for Europe and Africa, and one for Oceania. The format was still two round-robin group stages, but with six groups of four followed by four groups of three. The group winners from round two advanced to a semifinal knockout stage, which Italy won.

The Final 32

In Mexico in 1986, the second round was played as a knockout stage rather than as a group stage. Therefore, along with the top two teams in each first-round group, the four best third-place teams also advanced. Argentina won title number two that year.

The format of the World Cup remained unchanged through 1994. Then in 1998 for the tournament in France, the field expanded yet again, this time to the current 32 teams and the present format. The teams are drawn into eight groups of four for a round-robin in round one. The top two teams in each group then advance to a 16-team knockout stage.

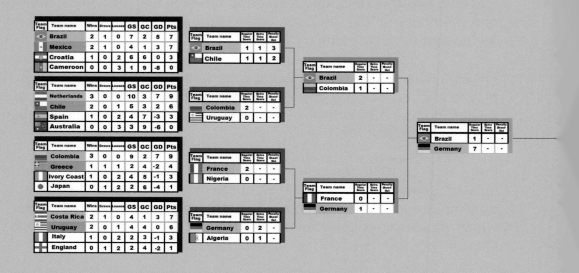

Big Expansion Plans

As the soccer played around the world continues to improve year after year, there is a growing need to give **emerging** countries a better chance to be represented on the sport's biggest stage. There is, however, a counterargument that expansion dilutes the quality of the World Cup by bringing down the average level of play as weaker teams will fill out the added spots.

Both sides of this debate were very vocal in January of 2017 when FIFA unanimously approved its plan to expand its **showcase** event by more teams than ever before—adding a whopping 16 spots, beginning with the 2026 World Cup. The hosts will likely be the United States, Canada, and Mexico in a joint bid, with the great majority of the games being played in the United States.

The proposed format is for 16 three-team groups, so be prepared to discuss Group P as a possible group of death. The top two in each group would still survive to advance to a 32-team knockout stage, which essentially means adding another round. This also means that there will

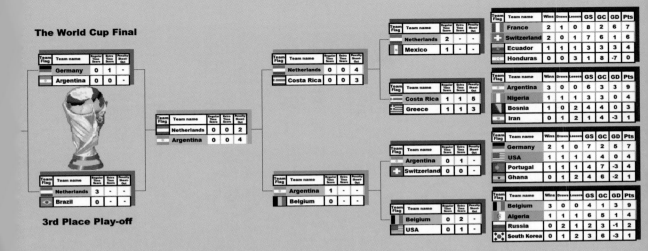

The World Cup Final tournament will expand from its current 32-team format to include 48 teams in 2026

be 80 matches rather than the current 64. FIFA insists that they can still pull off the expanded tournament in the same 32 days using the same 10 to 12 venues it uses for the current-sized event.

Critics are quick to point out that there are plenty of cons to this plan besides quality of play. One is that three-team groups can lead to unwanted situations. For example, Team A beats Team B, and Team B then draws with Team C. Team A has 3 points and teams B and C have 1 point each. In the remaining match between A and C, if no one tries particularly hard and the teams draw 0–0, both A and C advance, with Team C having zero wins and possibly zero goals. Meanwhile, Team B is left out in

FIFA president Gianni Infantino was elected to his position in large part due to his promise to expand the number of teams in the World Cup

Fans attending the World Cup in Mexico in 1986 saw the format switch from group play to a knockout stage in the second round

the cold and the fans are stuck with a stinker of a match. It is a scenario that will be nearly impossible to avoid.

There has also been criticism that the expansion of the World Cup was motivated more by FIFA president Gianni Infantino's desire to be elected in 2016 than by a desire to improve the tournament. Infantino ran for the job with expansion as his main platform, a position that was guaranteed to be popular with the underrepresented confederations—which were ones that had plenty of voting members. The promise he made to increase FIFA payments to member associations did not hurt his chances, either. It is also estimated that a bigger tournament will generate an extra billion dollars in revenue, which some say was the price that has been paid to give up a quality tournament.

SIDEBAR: PROPOSED 48-TEAM DISTRIBUTION

The chart below shows where the 16 added teams would come from when the World Cup expands in 2026. Europe will get three more teams and Africa four more. Oceania will be guaranteed a spot and no longer need to go to a playoff. The playoff will be between Asia and CONCACAF for the extra team. Both confederations will be guaranteed at least three more teams. CONMEBOL gets two more guaranteed teams.

UEFA	16 (13 CURRENTLY)
CAF	9 (5)
AFC	8.5 (4.5)
CONMEBOL	6 (4.5)
CONCACAF	6.5 (3.5)
OCEANIA	1 (0.5)
HOST COUNTRY	1 OR MORE IF CO-HOSTED (1)

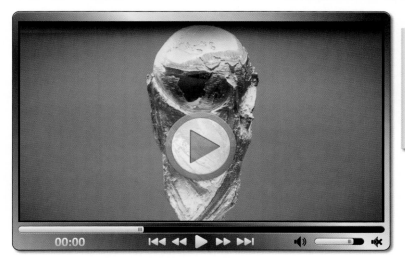

00:00

Here is a summary of the World Cup expansion plan

Mensur Mujdža (#13) of Bosnia and Herzegovina fends off two Argentina players in the first-ever World Cup match for his country in 2014. With expansion to 48 teams, many more countries will have a real opportunity to qualify for the first time

Infantino, however, knew where the votes were, and argued for a different, more globally inclusive look for the sport. "We are in the 21st century, and we have to shape the football World Cup of the 21st century. Football is more than just Europe and South America. Football is global," Infantino said.

Fans of the expansion agreed. After all, assuming a lower quality of play means assuming that the nations that will be included in 2026 will not improve in a decade, which is not a certainty by any means. The expanded format also adds an entire round of knockout matches, which always carry the possibility of high drama.

Certainly, engaging another 16 nations' worth of fans can only heighten the interest in the planet's most popular sporting event. Even qualifying rounds become more interesting as many teams will have their chances of making it to the World Cup greatly enhanced. For many of these nations, qualification in 2026 will mean their first-ever appearance at soccer's biggest event.

Once at the tournament, the chance to advance beyond the group stage is also much greater, as 32 teams make it through to the knockout stage. As to the argument that that politics and money drove FIFA to dilute the World Cup, if fans are truly not interested in watching Germany play the ninth qualifier from Asia or Africa, then they have the option of not buying tickets and not tuning in. That result would give FIFA pause to reconsider the decision. Somehow, it is difficult to imagine that even the toughest of critics believe that outcome is likely.

Logistics will be an issue with 48 competing teams. How many host nations can provide 48 acceptable training and practice facilities? In the case of a joint US-Canada-Mexico bid, this is a non-issue, which is another reason why that bid has a leg up. Mexico has hosted the World Cup before on two occasions. It first hosted in1970, then again in 1986 after Colombia dropped out as host. The United States, of course, hosted in 1994. Both countries showed the ability to easily handle hosting on their own. Joining forces, and then also adding a third partner in Canada, would certainly eliminate any capacity concerns arising from accommodating the additional 16 teams. For smaller nations with weaker infrastructure, however, the challenge is very real, and may provide an extra obstacle to certain prospective hosts.

SIDEBAR: ROCKING THE JOINT

The only time FIFA has allowed a joint bid, otherwise known as having two countries bid to share hosting duties for a single World Cup tournament, was in 2002. That year, Japan and South Korea bid to host the event together. More than a decade after that experience and a decision to hold off on more joint bids, FIFA announced in 2016 that it would once again entertain the idea of co-hosts for its flagship tournament.

That decision sparked serious conversations between the soccer federations of the United States and Mexico at the 2016 FIFA Congress. Both nations were considering individual bids for the 2026 event. It was widely speculated that a North American country would get the bid as USA 1994 was the last time the World Cup was hosted on the continent. The news that joint bids would once again be considered prompted the two would-be competitors to discuss pooling their resources.

Discussions continued throughout the year, and the decision was made to include Canada, as the Canadians were also considering making a bid after successfully hosting the Women's World Cup in 2015. In December of 2016, CONCACAF president Victor Montagliani announced the possibility of a three-way bid.

In July of 2017, the United Bid Committee was officially formed, and with the expansion to a 48-team format, the strength of the bid shared by countries that had all hosted World Cup events on their own was obvious. In its proposal, the USA will host 60 matches, with Canada and Mexico hosting 10 each. All matches from the quarterfinals on will be hosted in the United States. With the deadline for announcing the intention to bid for the 2026 event just a month away, it appeared the joint North American bid would go unopposed.

Just hours before the deadline, however, Morocco announced its intention to submit a competing bid. Morocco has bid unsuccessfully for the 1994, 1998, 2006, and 2010 World Cups. Given the haste of this decision, the massive domestic television revenues possible in both Mexico and the United States, and the superiority of the existing North American infrastructure, the joint bid is a heavy favorite. It will be very surprising if the first match of the 2026 World Cup does not kick off on American shores.

Will the new expanded format be a boom or a bust? FIFA has bet heavily that more countries and more revenue will be better for both fans and the sport. After the summer of 2026, the hope is that everyone will be asking why they did not expand the World Cup sooner. Or perhaps the talk will be about when they plan to expand again. The waiting has just begun.

This practice field at Wits University in Johannesburg was one of the facilities used for training and practice during the 2010 World Cup in South Africa. For small prospective host nations, providing these facilities for 48 teams may be a difficult challenge to meet

TEXT-DEPENDENT QUESTIONS:

1. How many teams qualified for the 1954 World Cup in Switzerland?

2. When did FIFA unanimously approve the plan to expand the World Cup to 48 teams, starting in 2026?

3. When was Gianni Infantino elected FIFA president?

RESEARCH PROJECT:

Another wildly successful sports tournament is the NCAA (National Collegiate Athletic Association) men's basketball tournament. Keeping in mind the history of the World Cup and its evolving format, read up on the way that the NCAA tournament has expanded over the years and weigh up its successes and failures. Then write a report about how you think the new World Cup expansion will fare by drawing parallels with the case of the NCAA tournament.

Advantage: when a player is fouled but play is allowed to continue because the team that suffered the foul is in a better position than they would have been had the referee stopped the game.

Armband: removable colored band worn around the upper arm by a team's captain, to signify that role.

Bend: skill attribute in which players strike the ball in a manner that applies spin, resulting in the flight of the ball curving, or bending, in mid-air.

Bicycle kick: a specific scoring attempt made by a player with their back to the goal. The player throws their body into the air, makes a shearing movement with the legs to get one leg in front of the other, and attempts to play the ball backwards over their own head, all before returning to the ground. Also known as an *overhead kick.*

Box: common name for the penalty area, a rectangular area measuring 44 yards (40.2 meters) by 18 yards (16.5 meters) in front of each goal. Fouls occurring within this area result in a penalty kick.

Club: collective name for a team, and the organization that runs it.

CONCACAF: acronym for the *Confederation of North, Central American and Caribbean Association Football*, the governing body of the sport in North and Central America and the Caribbean; pronounced "kon-ka-kaff."

CONMEBOL: acronym for the South American Football Association, the governing body of the sport in South America; pronounced "kon-me-bol."

Corner kick: kick taken from within a 1-yard radius of the corner flag; a method of restarting play when a player plays the ball over their own goal line without a goal being scored.

Cross: delivery of the ball into the penalty area by the attacking team, usually from the area between the penalty box and the touchline.

Dead ball: situation when the game is restarted with the ball stationary; i.e., a free kick.

Defender: one of the four main positions in soccer. Defenders are positioned in front of the goalkeeper and have the principal role of keeping the opposition away from their goal.

Dribbling: when a player runs with the ball at their feet under close control.

Flag: small rectangular flag attached to a handle, used by an assistant referee to signal that they have seen a foul or other infraction take place. "The flag is up" is a common expression for when the assistant referee has signaled for an offside.

Flick-on: when a player receives a pass from a teammate and, instead of controlling it, touches the ball with their head or foot while it is moving past them, with the intent of helping the ball reach another teammate.

Forward: one of the four main positions in football. Strikers are the players closest to the opposition goal, with the principal role of scoring goals. Also known as a *striker* or *attacker*.

Free kick: the result of a foul outside the penalty area given against the offending team. Free kicks can be either direct (shot straight toward the goal) or indirect (the ball must touch another player before a goal can be scored).

Fullback: position on either side of the defense, whose job is to try to prevent the opposing team attacking down the wings.

Full-time: the end of the game, signaled by the referees whistle. Also known as the *final whistle*.

Goal difference: net difference between goals scored and goals conceded. Used to differentiate league or group stage positions when clubs are tied on points.

Goalkeeper: one of the four main positions in soccer. This is the player closest to the goal a team is defending. They are the only player on the pitch that can handle the ball in open play, although they can only do so in the penalty area.

Goal kick: method of restarting play when the ball is played over the goal line by a player of the attacking team without a goal being scored.

Goal-line technology: video replay or sensor technology systems used to determine whether the ball has crossed the line for a goal or not.

Hat trick: when a player scores three goals in a single match.

Header: using the head as a means of playing or controlling the ball.

Linesman: another term for the assistant referee that patrols the sideline with a flag monitoring play for fouls, offsides, and out of bounds.

Long ball: attempt to distribute the ball a long distance down the field without the intention to pass it to the feet of the receiving player.

Manager: the individual in charge of the day-to-day running of the team. Duties of the manager usually include overseeing training sessions, designing tactical plays, choosing the team's formation, picking the starting eleven, and making tactical switches and substitutions during games.

Man of the Match: an award, often decided by pundits or sponsors, given to the best player in a game.

Midfielder: one of the four main positions in soccer. Midfielders are positioned between the defenders and forwards.

OFC: initials for the *Oceania Football Confederation*, the governing body of the sport in Oceania.

Offside: a player is offside if they are in their opponent's half of the field and closer to the goal line than both the second-last defender and the ball at the moment the ball is played to them by a teammate. Play is stopped and a free kick is given against the offending team.

Offside trap: defensive tactical maneuver, in which each member of a team's defense will simultaneously step forward as the ball is played forward to an opponent, in an attempt to put that opponent in an offside position.

Own goal: where a player scores a goal against their own team, usually as the result of an error.

Penalty area: rectangular area measuring 44 yards (40.2 meters) by 18 yards (16.5 meters) in front of each goal; commonly called *the box*.

Penalty kick: kick taken 12 yards (11 meters) from goal, awarded when a team commits a foul inside its own penalty area.

Penalty shootout: method of deciding a match in a knockout competition, which has ended in a draw after full-time and extra-time. Players from each side take turns to attempt to score a penalty kick against the opposition goalkeeper. Sudden death is introduced if scores are level after each side has taken five penalties.

Red card: awarded to a player for either a single serious cautionable offence or following two yellow cards. The player receiving the red card is compelled to leave the game for the rest of its duration, and that player's team is not allowed to replace him with another player. A player receiving the red card is said to have been *sent off* or *ejected*.

Side: another word for team.

Stoppage time: an additional number of minutes at the end of each half, determined by the match officials, to compensate for time lost during the game. Informally known by various names, including *injury time* and *added time*.

Striker: see Forward.

Studs: small points on the underside of a player's boots to help prevent slipping. A tackle in which a player directs their studs toward an opponent is referred to as a *studs-up challenge*, and is a foul punishable by a red card.

Substitute: a player who is brought on to the pitch during a match in exchange for a player currently in the game.

Sweeper: defender whose role is to protect the space between the goalkeeper and the rest of the defense.

Tackle: method of a player winning the ball back from an opponent, achieved either by using the feet to take possession from the opponent, or making a slide tackle to knock the ball away. A tackle in which the opposing player is kicked before the ball is punishable by either a free kick or penalty kick. Dangerous tackles may also result in a yellow or red card.

Throw-in: method of restarting play. Involves a player throwing the ball from behind a touch line after an opponent has kicked it out.

Trap: skill performed by a player, whereupon the player uses their foot (or, less commonly, their chest or thigh) to bring an airborne or falling ball under control.

UEFA: acronym for *Union of European Football Associations*, the governing body of the sport in Europe; pronounced "you-eh-fa."

Winger: wide midfield player whose primary focus is to provide crosses into the penalty area. Alternatively known as a *wide midfielder*.

World Cup: commonly refers to the men's FIFA World Cup tournament held every four years, but is also associated with the FIFA Women's World Cup, international tournaments for youth football, (such as the FIFA U-20 World Cup), and the FIFA Club World Cup.

Yellow card: shown by the referee to a player who commits a cautionable offence. If a player commits two cautionable offences in a match, they are shown a second yellow card, followed by a red card, and are then sent off. Also known as a *caution* or a *booking*.

FURTHER READING, INTERNET RESOURCES & VIDEO CREDITS:

Further Reading:

Bader, Bonnie. *What is the World Cup? (What Was?)*. New York, NY: Penguin Publishing Group, 2018.

Radnedge, Keir. *World Soccer Records 2015*. London, UK: Carlton Books, 2015.

Jökulsson, Illugi. *Stars of the World Cup (World Soccer Legends)*. New York, NY: Abbeville Kids, 2014.

Internet Resources:

FIFA: www.fifa.com

UEFA: www.uefa.com

CONCACAF: www.concacaf.com

Video Credits:

Chapter 1:
Cristiano Ronaldo of Portugal is one of UEFA's and the world's top players, as demonstrated in this highlight reel:
http://x-qr.net/1CuY

Chapter 2:
Watch club teammates Neymar and Luis Suarez battle as captains for opposing teams in a 2018 CONMEBOL World Cup-qualifying match in Brazil:
http://x-qr.net/1DtU

Chapter 3:
Watch the highlights of the match between 1998 World Cup group of death survivors England and Romania:
http://x-qr.net/1Da0

Chapter 4:
Watch the teenage brilliance of England's Michael Owen at the 1998 World Cup:
http://x-qr.net/1FWo

Chapter 5:
Here is a summary of the World Cup expansion plan:
http://x-qr.net/1GBy

INDEX

INDEX

Andrew Luke

ABOUT THE AUTHOR:

Andrew Luke is a former journalist, reporting on both sports and general news for many years at television stations in various locations across the US affiliated with NBC, CBS and Fox. Prior to his journalism career he worked with the Boston Red Sox Major League baseball team. An avid writer and sports enthusiast, he has authored 26 other books on sports topics. In his downtime Andrew enjoys family time with his wife and two young children and attending hockey and baseball games in his home city of Pittsburgh, PA.

PICTURE CREDITS: